LEGENDS OF WARFARE

AVIATION

Consolidated B-24, Vol.1

The XB-24 to B-24E Liberators in World War II

DAVID DOYLE

Schiffer Publishing Ltd

4880 Lower Valley Road • Atglen, PA 19310

Other Schiffer Books on Related Subjects:
Grumman F4F Wildcat by David Doyle (978-0-7643-5433-5)
Curtiss P-40 Warhawk by David Doyle (978-0-7643-5432-8)
Bell 47/H-13 Sioux Helicopter by Wayne Mutza (978-0-7643-5376-5)

Designed by Justin Watkinson
Type set in Impact/Minion Pro/Univers LT Std

ISBN: 978-0-7643-5615-5
Printed in China

Published by Schiffer Publishing, Ltd.
4880 Lower Valley Road
Atglen, PA 19310
Phone: (610) 593-1777; Fax: (610) 593-2002
E-mail: Info@schifferbooks.com
www.schifferbooks.com

For our complete selection of fine books on this and related subjects, please visit our website at www.schifferbooks.com. You may also write for a free catalog.

Schiffer Publishing's titles are available at special discounts for bulk purchases for sales promotions or premiums. Special editions, including personalized covers, corporate imprints, and excerpts, can be created in large quantities for special needs. For more information, contact the publisher.

We are always looking for people to write books on new and related subjects. If you have an idea for a book, please contact us at proposals@schifferbooks.com.

Acknowledgments

I have been blessed with the generous help of many friends and colleagues when preparing this manuscript. Truly, this book would not have been possible without their collective assistance. Tom Kailbourn, Stan Piet, Scott Taylor, Dana Bell, Brett Stolle, and Sarah Swan at the National Museum of the United States Air Force, all gave of their time without hesitation. My lovely and dear wife, Denise, scanned photos, proofread manuscripts, and was my personal cheerleader throughout the difficult parts of this project, and without her unflagging support this could not have been completed.

All photos from the collection of the National Museum of the United States Air Force, unless otherwise noted.

Contents

Introduction

Boeing's 1935 B-17 Flying Fortress design gave the United States its first production heavy bomber. Seeking to expand production of the B-17, in 1938, the Army Air Corps asked that Consolidated evaluate the B-17 and issue a proposal to build the Flying Fortress under license.

Following an examination not only of the B-17, but also the Boeing production methodology, Consolidated countered the Air Corps request that they instead produce a new heavy bomber possessing greater range, higher ceiling, and higher speed than the B-17, whose design dated to 1935.

In January 1939, the Air Corps, indicating an agreement to Consolidated's counter offer, issued specification C-212, basically copying the criteria that Consolidated had issued with their new design, which they had designated as Model 32.

Central to the design of the Model 32 was the shoulder-mounted high aspect-ratio Davis wing. This type of airfoil had previously been used on the Consolidated Model 31, the XP4Y Corregidor. Designer David R. Davis had engineered this airfoil section to mimic the shape of a raindrop. Davis, who was not a Consolidated employee, had offered company president Reuben Fleet a license to use his wing design for a fee of $2,500 plus .5% of the sales price, less government furnished equipment, of any aircraft incorporating his wing design.

While indeed the Davis wing of the B-24 was very aerodynamically efficient at the speeds the B-24 would operate in, the B-24 had less wing area than did the B-17, despite a six-foot increase in wingspan. As a result, wing loadings were higher; in practice this resulted in some unpleasant flight characteristics when the bomber was heavily laden and operating at high altitudes.

In addition to the Davis wing upon which were mounted four engines, the Model 32 sported dual vertical stabilizers, and two bomb bays closed by all-metal, roll-type bomb bay doors.

The B-24, dubbed the Liberator as a result of a naming contest amongst Consolidated employees, would go on to become not only the most-produced bomber of World War II, but also the most-produced US military aircraft of all time.

On March 30, 1939, the Army contracted with Consolidated to construct a single XB-24 prototype, stipulating that the aircraft had to be delivered before the end of the year. Work began in earnest to meet that deadline.

The XB-24 was ready for its first flight on December 29, 1939. The aircraft that rolled out of Consolidated's San Diego plant was the first production heavy bomber to use tricycle landing gear, and featured a "wet" wing. Virtually the entire Davis wing was a fuel tank. Four 14-cylinder twin-row Pratt & Whitney R-1830-33 Twin Wasp radial engines powered the aircraft. Each engine was equipped with mechanical two-speed superchargers, and was rated at 1,000 horsepower.

Consolidated's chief test pilot Bill Wheatley was at the controls for the December 29 maiden flight, which was taken with the twin rudder assembly literally borrowed from the single Consolidated Model 31. In early 1940, the XB-24 was ferried to Wright Field, Ohio, for testing and evaluation. The aircraft initially was assigned serial number 39-556, but that was later corrected to 39-680. The aircraft had provision for mounting six .30-caliber machine guns, none of which were in turrets.

The initial testing revealed several deficiencies, chief of which was the inability of the XB-24 to attain the promised top speed. While the specification called for a maximum speed of 311 miles per hour, the XB-24 could attain only 273 mph. In an effort to remedy this, the R-1830-33s with their mechanically driven superchargers were replaced first with R-1830-41s sporting General Electric B-2 turbosuperchargers, and still later with turbosupercharged R-1830-43 engines.

Simultaneously, the borrowed Model 31 tail assembly was replaced with a two-foot-wider model, and the pitot tubes relocated from the wings to the nose. The aircraft was redesignated XB-24B, and with the improvements could attain 310 MPH. The aircraft was later converted to a VIP transport operated by Consairway for the Air Corps Ferrying Command. Following World War II, the XB-24 was scrapped at Brookley Field, Mobile, Alabama, on June 20, 1946.

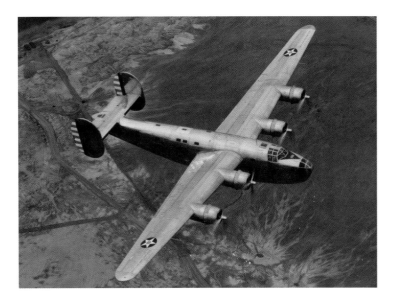

The prototype or pilot for the Liberator bombers was the one-off Consolidated XB-24, US Army Air Corps (USAAC) serial number 39-556, produced under Contract 12436. Designated the Model 32 by the manufacturer, its key features were a stubby nose, twin vertical fins and rudders, and the Davis wings, designed by David R. Davis. These wings had a teardrop-shaped cross section and had a high aspect ratio, meaning the wings were quite long with respect to their mean chord. The XB-24 was powered by four 1,200-horsepower Pratt & Whitney R-1830-33 (S3C4-G) Twin Wasp 14-cylinder radial engines equipped with mechanical two-speed superchargers. Its first flight was on December 29, 1939, with Consolidated's chief test pilot Bill Wheatley at the controls. As built, the XB-24 had five wing slots, outboard of the national insignia on each wing, and these are visible here.

Cruising below cloud cover, the XB-24 is viewed from its lower front right quarter. The plane was equipped with two bomb bays, with large bomb-bay doors extending up the sides of the fuselage to the lower wing roots; those doors are visible in this photograph. "U.S." is marked in black under the right wing and "ARMY" under the left wing. The XB-24 had a pitot tube on the leading edge of each wing, about midway between the outer engine nacelle and the wing tip.

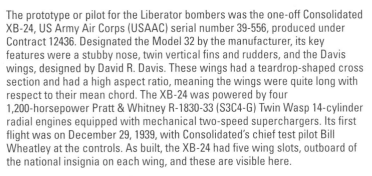

The Consolidated XB-24 is in low-level flight, showing its tricycle landing gear lowered. At this time, the plane had a highly polished bare-aluminum finish, with horizontal red and white stripes and a vertical blue stripe on the rudder. Note how the tail of the fuselage was even with the trailing edges of the elevators.

The XB-24 is on a hardstand, with a tow line from the plane attached to the tractor to the left. This photo was taken before the plane received the upgraded R-1830-41 engines with General Electric B-2 turbosuperchargers during 1940. With these changes, along with the elimination of the wing slots, and the addition of self-sealing fuel tanks and redesigned cowlings with an oil cooler inlet on each side, the XB-24 was redesignated the XB-24B.

CHAPTER 2
YB-24 and LB-30A

Even before the XB-24 was completed, the Air Corps had issued a contract for additional test aircraft. Seven of these service test aircraft, designated YB-24, were ordered on April 27, 1939. The aircraft were originally assigned serial numbers 39-681 to 39-687, but due to changing requirements these were later changed to 40-696 through 40-702.

Even though the testing XB-24 had not yet been completed, there was to be some refinement in the design of the YB-24 aircraft. One of these was the deletion of the five slots in the outer end of each wing, making the YB-24 consistent with the revamped XB-24B in this regard.

Further, drawing on experience being gained in high-altitude operations with the Davis wing, deicer boots were added on the leading edges of the wings and tail surfaces. While the XB-24B had attained 310 miles per hour top speed (close to the 311 mph called for in the specifications), the addition of the deicer boots, as well as camouflage paint, resulted in the top speed of the YB-24 dropping back to 275 mph. Like the XB-24, the YB-24 had a bomb capacity of 8,000 pounds.

While seven YB-24 aircraft were ordered on contract 12464, in reality only one was delivered as such to the Army Air Corps. The remaining six aircraft on the order were diverted for sale to the British, who were already immersed in World War II. This direct purchase (the transaction predated Lend-Lease) was authorized on November 9, 1940, under contract F-677. The aircraft were designated by the British as LB-30A, derived from a French designation, and were assigned RAF serial numbers AM258 through AM263.

The aircraft, designated Liberator GR by the British, were modified for British service in Montreal. While the lack of self-sealing fuel tanks caused the British to deem them unfit for combat use, they were employed by the Atlantic Return Ferry Service as transports. This service transported RAF pilots to Canada, where the pilots would pick up new military aircraft and fly them to England.

However, this sale did not reduce the number of aircraft that the Army Air Corps had on order, it merely allowed the British request to take precedence over the US production. To make up the delivery shortage of the YB-24s, six additional B-24Ds were delivered to the USAAC. These aircraft were assigned the YB-24 serial numbers 40-696 through 40-701. The only YB-24 actually delivered as such was 40-702. This aircraft was assigned by the USAAC to the Consolidated plant, where it was used for testing. It was later redesignated RB-24 (R for restricted service). It was written off at MacDill Field, Florida, on March 28, 1944.

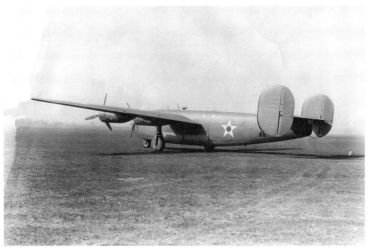

Before the first flight of the XB-24, the US Army Air Corps ordered seven YB-24 service-test airplanes. These were assigned USAAC serial numbers 40-696 to 40-702. However, the first six YB-24s, which were produced under Contract A-5068, were instead delivered to the British, with only 40-702, which was produced under Contract 12464, remaining in the US service. That aircraft, which later was redesignated B-24 (with no letter suffix) is shown here. The YB-24 was similar to the XB-24, except the wing slots were deleted, and deicer boots were installed on the leading edges of the wings and the vertical fins.

Consolidated YB-24 serial number 40-702 is viewed from the left rear. In the tail of the fuselage was a station for a machine gunner, with sliding doors though which a hand-controlled machine gun could be brought into play. On the deck of the fuselage above the wings is a "football" radio direction-finding antenna. This YB-24 was equipped with self-sealing fuel tanks and crew armor.

YB-24 serial number 40-702 is observed from the front. Note the strut braces on the outboard sides of the main landing gear. The main gear, when retracted, pivoted outward into wells in the bottoms of the wings. The propellers on the early B-24s were three-bladed. The light-colored discs to the rear of the propeller hubs were permanent fixtures and may have been the base plates for propeller spinners, sometimes present on the YB-24 but absent here.

Six of the seven Consolidated YB-24s were diverted to the British, who designated these bombers LB-30A, assigning them RAF serial numbers AM258 to AM263. The British used the LB-30As as personnel transports, primarily in the Canada-to-UK routes. The conversions to transports were performed in Montreal, Canada. *Stan Piet collection*

The last of the six British LB-30As derived from YB-24s, RAF serial number AM263, runs up its engines at an unidentified air base, while a ground crewman scampers alongside the open bomb bay. Below the small window to the rear of the glass nose is the right pitot tube. Whereas the XB-24 had a pitot tube on each wing, the YB-24 and the LB-30As had a pitot tube in the position shown here and also on the opposite side of the nose.

The two pitot tubes on the sides of the nose of the LB-30A are seen to good advantage in this frontal photograph. Landing lights are on the leading edges of both wings, between the inboard and the outboard engine nacelles.

An LB-30A, most likely RAF serial number AM263, is viewed from aft with its engines running, permitting a good view of the tail machine-gun position. Below the two windows just below the horizontal stabilizer are two curved, sliding doors, shown in the closed position. To operate the manually controlled machine gun, the doors were slid open and the machine gun was moved into firing position.

One of the LB-30s converted from YB-24s to personnel transports flies above Manhattan. It was painted in the RAF camouflage scheme of Dark Earth and Dark Green over Black. The matte black deicer boots are visible on the leading edges of the wings. These were rubber covers that were slightly inflated to break up ice buildup on the wings. *Stan Piet collection*

Consolidated LB-30A RAF serial number AM262 flies high above farmlands. The wing roundels are blue and red, while the fuselage roundels are red, white, blue, and yellow. Fin flashes are red, white, and blue. Note the rectangular windows and the escape hatch with a window aft of the wing. *Stan Piet collection*

The British LB-30As saw service as personnel transports with the Atlantic Return Ferry Service. Pilots who flew warplanes from bases in eastern Canada to the UK were ferried back to Canada by way of the Atlantic Return Ferry Service. *Stan Piet collection*

CHAPTER 3
Liberator I

France, desperate for warplanes, had ordered 120 of the big Consolidated bombers even before the XB-24 was complete. These aircraft were intended to equip the *Armée de l'Air*, but when France fell, the aircraft were instead scheduled for delivery to the British.

By the time production of the aircraft began, the design of the B-24A had been finalized, and it was upon this design the British, formerly French-destined, production was based. Because at the time the French placed the order, that nation was at war, the US Army Air Corps allowed the first twenty B-24A aircraft on order by the US, serial numbers 40-2349 through 40-2386, to be diverted to France, and thus on to Britain.

As previously mentioned, the YB-24s had been delivered to the British, who designated them LB-30A. The former French aircraft were accordingly designated LB-30B, or in RAF parlance, Liberator I. The RAF assigned the aircraft serial numbers AM910 through AM929. As had been the case with the LB-30A, the R-1830-33-powered Liberator Is were delivered to Montreal, Canada. However, because the order was transferred to Britain before the aircraft were actually built, they were delivered with British-configured armament of six machine guns, one in the nose, one in the belly, two in the tail, and one each in the waist position.

However, once the aircraft arrived in England, many of the Liberator Is were heavily modified in order to adapt them to a role the RAF felt them well-suited for: combating U-boats. The long-range capabilities of the Liberator, as well as its expansive bomb load, lent it to use by the RAF Coastal Command. Dispatched to Heston Aircraft, the Liberators were there equipped with Air-to-Surface Vessel (ASV) radar and Yagi antennas for search purposes, while beneath the fuselage was mounted a packet of four Hispano 20 mm automatic cannons.

Upon completion of modifications, the Liberator Is were assigned to No.120 Squadron, where they served until December 1943. The long range of the aircraft allowed the RAF to close the so-called Mid-Atlantic Gap, a portion of the sea that was previously beyond the range of antisubmarine patrols.

One Liberator I, AM927, was never delivered to the RAF. This aircraft was damaged in transit, and was returned to Consolidated. During repair, four feet were added to its nose, making the nose configuration similar to that of later models, while the canopy and remainder of the aircraft was consistent with the early models. That aircraft survives today, flying as "Diamond Lil" with the Commemorative Air Force.

The British ordered twenty examples of the Liberator I, which they assigned RAF serial numbers AM910 to AM929. These were produced between March and June 1941, under Contract F-677. These planes retained the short nose of the YB-24/LB-30A. The majority of these twenty Liberator Is were assigned to Coastal Command, while four were delivered to British Overseas Aircraft Company (BOAC). The Liberator I shown here was likely RAF serial number AM910, having been outfitted for antisubmarine work by Scottish Aviation Ltd. in the summer of 1941. Antennas for the Air-to-Surface Vessel (ASV) radar are atop and on the sides of the aft fuselage and under the wings, while under the forward fuselage is a gondola containing four fixed, forward-firing 20 mm cannons. *Imperial War Museum*

Liberator I serial number AM910 is viewed from the right side. At the time this photo was taken in July 1941, AM910 was undergoing tests at the Aeroplane and Armament Experimental Establishment, at Boscombe Down, England. This aircraft was transferred to 120 Squadron on September 5, 1941. *Imperial War Museum*

A Liberator I skims over the ocean during a transatlantic flight. Sources vary over the RAF serial number of this airplane, some stating that it was AM922 and at least one other affirming that it was AM929, the final Liberator I: only "AM92" is visible on the rear fuselage. *Imperial War Museum*

Liberator I AM920 is being prepared for takeoff at Prestwick, Scotland, during March 1942. Later, this was one of the Liberator Is transferred to BOAC, where it flew under civil registration number G-AHYB. It had the honor, in February 1946, of flying BOAC's 2,000th Atlantic crossing. Still later, this aircraft was transferred to the French, and it served as the personal airplane of Emperor Báo Đại of Indochina.
Imperial War Museum

Twenty-nine B-24A aircraft were ordered by the US Army Air Corps even before the XB-24 first took flight. As discussed in the previous chapter, the bulk of the B-24A production, twenty aircraft, were delivered to Britain as Liberator Mk.Is. The balance of the order, serial numbers 40-2368 through 40-2377, however were delivered to the US Army Air Corps. The aircraft were delivered between June 16 and July 10, 1941.

The armament of these aircraft differed from that of their Britain-bound cousins in being equipped with four .50-caliber machine guns in the nose, waist, and belly positions. A pair of .30-caliber machine guns were in the tail to ward off attack from the rear.

The aircraft were delivered in RAF-style camouflage of Dark Earth and Dark Green over Black, but to clearly distinguish the American planes, as the US was a neutral nation when the B-24As were delivered, large American flags were painted on either side of the nose as well as atop the fuselage.

Two of these aircraft, serial numbers 40-2373 and 40-2374, were used to fly the Harriman-Beaverbrook mission to Moscow to negotiate unconditional aid for the Soviet Union in September 1941.

Two other examples of the type had been selected for use on a secret spy mission over Japanese bases on Jaluit and Truk, prior to the US entry in World War II. The cover story, if detected, was to be that the aircraft got lost while flying to the Philippines. However, before the flight could take place, the Japanese attacked Pearl Harbor, coincidentally destroying 40-2371, one of the planes being prepared for this mission, on the ground at Hickam Field.

Three further of the nine B-24As built were destroyed by the Japanese in combat, while one, 40-2376 ditched off Ju Island on May 5, 1942, while being operated by the Air Transport Command. Two aircraft, 40-2369 and 40-2375, were operated by Consairway and survived the war. They were subsequently scrapped at Kingman, Arizona, and Walnut Ridge, Arkansas, respectively.

Only nine B-24As were produced as such, and they were delivered to the US Army Air Corps, in June and July 1941. The Army assigned to them serial numbers 40-2369 to 40-2377. The example shown here is the next-to-last B-24A, with the number "76" on the tail. Large American flags were painted on the fuselage as part of US efforts to assert its official status of neutrality. RAF-type camouflage of Dark Green and Dark Earth over Black was applied to the aircraft. *Stan Piet collection*

As seen in a photo of a B-24A in flight, this model was similar in exterior details to the B-24/Liberator I, with its short nose and truncated tail with a compartment for a twin .30-caliber machine gun in lieu of a tail turret. The B-24As were classified as Restricted and thus redesignated (R)B-24A, and most of them served as transport aircraft with the Army Ferry Command. *Stan Piet collection*

This B-24A is painted in the standard Air Corps camouflage scheme of Olive Drab over Neutral Gray. To the front of the RDF "football" antenna on the top deck of the fuselage was a barely visible whip antenna, and to the front of that antenna was a short mast antenna. *Stan Piet collection*

The number 71 is stenciled over a dark-colored patch on the vertical fin of B-24A USAAC serial number 40-2371 in this view of the right rear of the plane. The national insignia are the type approved before May 1942, consisting of a white star on a blue circle, with a red circle inside the star. To the rear of the national insignia on the fuselage is the emblem of Ferry Command.

Flight crewmen and ground crewmen are gathered around B-24A serial number 40-2371, emblazoned with the oversized US flags employed in the months before the United States entered World War II. To the front of the flag and below the pitot tube is the aircraft's nomenclature, serial-number, and crew-weight stencil. On the upper front of the clear bombardier's nose is a small ball mount for a manually controlled machine gun. This aircraft was destroyed at Pearl Harbor on December 7, 1941.

CHAPTER 5
Liberator II

Visually, the Liberator II varied from the Liberator I chiefly in two respects: the Mk.II had an extended nose and tail, resulting in a fuselage that was two feet, seven inches longer than that of the Liberator I. In addition, these were the first Liberators equipped with turrets. Here, members of the flight crew of Liberator II, serial number AL574 and fuselage code "O," stand next to the plane at the airbase at Fayid, Egypt, during February 1942. *Imperial War Museum*

In 1941, the British ordered 165 examples of a new model, the Liberator II, to be produced directly for the British, and not from stocks redirected from the US Army Air Corps.

These aircraft could be readily distinguished from earlier models in that the nose of the Liberator II was extended two feet seven inches. Perhaps even more significantly, the Liberator II was equipped for the installation of power-operated gun turrets. Provisions were made for the installation of two Boulton-Paul turrets, each armed with four Browning .303-caliber machine guns. At the tail was a model E. Mk.II turret, while atop the fuselage just to the rear of the wing was a model A. Mk.IV. Only one of the Liberator IIs left the San Diego plant with the turrets installed. The intention was that the turrets on the remainder of the aircraft be installed in England, where the turrets were made.

The armament of these aircraft was further enhanced by flexible .303-caliber machine guns mounted in the nose and belly, and a pair fitted to each waist window. Drawing further on the lessons learned in combat, the Liberator Mk. II was equipped with self-sealing fuel tanks.

The very first Liberator Mk.II, RAF serial number AL503, made its maiden flight on May 26, 1941. A few days later, while on its acceptance flight on June 2, 1941, the bomber crashed into San Diego Bay, killing all five on board, including thirty-nine-year-old William Wheatley, Consolidated's chief test pilot, who was at the controls. Reports at the time blamed sabotage.

Interestingly, despite this, the second Liberator Mk.II, serial number AL504, would become Churchill's personal transport.

In the end, Consolidated delivered a total of 139 Liberator IIs to the RAF, which were assigned serial numbers AL503 to AL641, under Contract F-677. To make up for the lost AL503, the British received a US Army Air Force (USAAF) Liberator to which was assigned serial number FP685, under the same contract.

In the aftermath of the Japanese attack on Pearl Harbor, the USAAF commandeered part of the Liberator II production. Within the USAAF these aircraft were designated LB-30, which should not be confused with the ex-French LB-30A or the RAF LB-30B Liberator Is.

Some of those that did reach British hands were flown by the Coastal Command, while others were assigned to 159 Squadron (Middle East Detachment) and 160 Squadron. First based near the Suez Canal, as Rommel's forces began to draw near, the Liberators were withdrawn to bases in Palestine, from which they could strike Tobruk and Benghazi.

Liberator IIs served with several bomb squadrons, including Nos.159 and 160 Squadrons, RAF, and some were attached to No.511 Squadron, North Atlantic Return Ferry Service. This example, with 159 Squadron, is being prepared for a mission at Salbani, India, in 1943. On the top deck of the fuselage is a Boulton-Paul powered turret with four Browning .303-caliber machine guns. Faintly visible on the top deck aft of the cockpit are an astrodome and a loop-type radio direction-finding antenna. *Imperial War Museum*

A Liberator II from No.159 Squadron is being loaded with 500-pound general-purpose bombs at the airfield at Fayid, Egypt, in June 1943. The plane was painted matte black from the wings down, for camouflage during nighttime operations. Note the paint chipping down to the aluminum on the forward rim of the cowling to the right. *Imperial War Museum*

The serial number AL574 is faintly visible on the rear fuselage of a Liberator II of 159 Squadron while it is being bombed-up at Fayid, Egypt, in June 1943. Armorers are maneuvering a trailer full of 500-pound bombs. The trailer is equipped with two booms with manually operated bomb hoists. This is one of the Liberator IIs that was not armed with the Boulton-Paul tail and dorsal turrets. *Imperial War Museum*

"Marco Polo" is the name painted on the side of the fuselage of Liberator II AL578, assigned to No.45 Atlantic Transport Group and outfitted as a transport aircraft. It is being prepared for a transatlantic mission for the Return Ferry Service at Dorval, Montreal, Canada. To the left is a cart with markings for Royal Air Force Ferry command. *Imperial War Museum*

"Marco Polo," Liberator II AL578, is seen here in a bare-aluminum finish, with the code "HD" painted on the nose and the RAF serial number, AL578, painted on the bottom of the left wing. To the front of and below the "Marco Polo" inscription on the fuselage are what appear to be Chinese characters arranged vertically. *Imperial War Museum*

"Commando," Liberator II serial number AL504, was one of several aircraft that served as Prime Minister Winston Churchill's personal transport aircraft during World War II. It was stripped of all armaments and was equipped with upholstered seats, sleeping quarters, and a galley. "Commando" is shown following a 1943–44 overhaul, in which a solid nose, a single vertical tail, and a new horizontal stabilizer and elevators were installed. While ferrying several VIPs to Canada, "Commando" crashed into the Atlantic under mysterious circumstances on March 28, 1945. *Imperial War Museum*

CHAPTER 6
B-24C

The B-24C incorporated many improvements from previous models. It featured the extended nose, introduced with the Liberator II, as well as the turbosupercharged Pratt & Whitney R-1830-43 engines turning Hamilton Standard propellers as fitted to the XB-24B. The new engines, while bringing a marked improvement in performance, especially at altitudes above 20,000 feet, required revised cowlings. The redesigned elliptical cowlings would become a hallmark of future generations of Liberators.

Only nine examples of the B-24C were constructed, and they were to see use as test and crew training aircraft. Much of the testing involved armament and armor. The aircraft were delivered with a Martin 250CE-3 turret just behind the cockpit on top of the fuselage. An interrupter circuit stopped the guns from firing should the top turret gunner accidentally train the weapons on the tail surfaces of the B-24C.

Still further improvements were needed in armament, and while the aircraft were originally built with hand-operated twin tail machine guns, this area in particular needed improvement. At Eglin Field, Florida, at least one B-24C was equipped with a power tail turret, foreshadowing a characteristic that would be commonplace on future generations of B-24s. Building on the lessons learned, both in performance and manufacture, production soon switched to the B-24D, the first genuinely mass-produced, combat-ready Liberator. The B-24Cs were redesignated RB-24C, with the R designating "restricted from combat use."

Consolidated B-24C US Army Air Forces (USAAF) serial number 40-2384 was one of nine C-model Liberators completed under Contract 13281. The B-24Cs were called production-breakdown aircraft and served to prepare the assembly lines for full-scale production of combat-capable aircraft. Four turbosupercharged Pratt & Whitney R-1830-41 engines provided power for the B-24C, rated at 1,200 horsepower at 20,000 feet. The inclusion of air intakes on each side of the cowlings for the turbosuperchargers and intercoolers resulted in an elliptical shape for the fronts of the cowls, in contrast with round fronts on earlier models of the Liberator. The B-24C also had the extended nose, self-sealing fuel tanks, and, aft of the cockpit, a Martin Model 250CE-3 power-operated turret with twin .50-caliber machine guns.

Originally, the B-24Cs had a single machine gun in the nose. B-24C 40-2384 was modified with a cheek gun on each side of the nose. The nose is viewed from the left side, showing three .50-caliber machine guns in ball-and-socket mounts. In addition to the gun in the cheek window in the foreground, one is installed in the upper front of the nose, and the barrel of a gun mounted in the newly installed left cheek window is visible to the lower front of the nose.

The right cheek machine gun of B-24C 40-2384 is viewed close-up. The right .50-caliber cheek gun of this plane was mounted in a panel of the clear nose, not in a separate window as seen in the preceding photo of the left side of this plane's nose. The machine guns had the early-type, slotted cooling jackets over the barrels. Below the number "4" is stenciled "CREW CHIEFS," below which are three illegible names and ranks.

Although some B-24Cs were armed with the Consolidated Aircraft-designed A-6 power turret, at least one, serial number 40-2384, had a manually controlled twin .50-caliber machine-gun mount in the tail, as illustrated here from within the position. The guns had manual charging handles, flexible ammo feed chutes, ring sights, and twin grips, which are visible in the lower foreground.

The manually operated twin .50-caliber machine gun mount in the tail of a B-24C, presumably serial number 40-2384, is seen from farther forward than the preceding view. In the foreground are the two ammunition boxes for the guns. At the bottom center is a corrugated-metal catwalk.

CHAPTER 7

B-24D and PB4Y

Thanks in large part to their role in the famous Ploesti Raid, the B-24D for many is the iconic Liberator. The extended nose, introduced on the Liberator II, tipped with the multi-pane transparent bombardier's station, was used on the 2,738 B-24Ds produced. While all previous Liberators were built in San Diego, B-24D production was divided among three assembly plants, in what was known as the Liberator Production Pool. The bulk of B-24D production rolled off Consolidated's San Diego production, obviously already well established and prepared for B-24 production. In May 1942, additional B-24Ds began to leave the company's Fort Worth, Texas facility. While assembled in Texas, most of the components were produced by the San Diego plant. The two Consolidated plants were joined in production of the B-24D by Douglas Aircraft's Tulsa plant, which began building Liberators in July 1942.

Ultimately, San Diego built 2,425 B-24Ds, with Fort Worth adding 303, and Douglas built only ten before production in all three plants switched to B-24E model aircraft.

The B-24D was substantially better able to defend itself than were its predecessors. The Martin 250CE-3 turret introduced on the B-24C was retained, and was augmented by a Consolidated A-6A tail turret like the one tested on the B-24C at Eglin Field.

Initially, however, no ventral or waist armament was carried by the B-24D, but that was not long the case. Beginning with San Diego-produced B-24D-25-CO serial number 41-24220 as well as Fort Worth-built B-24D-10-CF, serial number 42-63837, a single flexible .50-caliber machine gun was added to the waist positions on either side of the bomber.

Starting with the seventy-seventh B-24D built, a retractable, remotely controlled, and sighted gun turret was installed. This turret housed a pair of .50-caliber machine guns. Such installations were stopped following the 287th example, owing to the difficulty of operating the weapon. A ventral tunnel, like that found on earlier Liberators, was introduced in the stead of the remote control turret. Finally, starting with B-24D-140-CO serial number 42-41164 a manned, retractable Sperry ball turret began to be installed, at last providing the Liberator with an effective under-aircraft defense.

In addition to the US Army Air Forces, the US Navy operated B-24Ds as well. All Navy Liberators came from contracts originally placed by the Army. The Navy aircraft were designated PB4Y-1, regardless of block number or even model number of the base aircraft, which spanned B-24D, G, J, L, and M models. The Navy's acquisition of and use of the Liberators, which they used for antisubmarine patrols, was a result of a deal negotiated for the use of the Navy-owned, Boeing-operated plant in Renton, Washington, which the Army wanted for B-29 production. Prior to this deal, the Navy had been denied authority to operate land-based bombers.

The first model of Liberator to enter large-scale production as a combat-ready aircraft was the B-24D. Similar in most respects to the B-24C, the D-model was built by the Liberator Production Pool, consisting of Consolidated's San Diego, California (CO), and Fort Worth, Texas (CF), plants and Douglas Aircraft's Tulsa, Oklahoma (DT), factory. The B-24Ds were built in many production blocks, numbered up to 170. For example, B-24D-5-DT was a Block 5 aircraft assembled at Douglas's Tulsa plant. Here, "Joisey Bounce," B-24D-25-CO serial number 41-24226, flies in formation with other B-24s assigned to the 93rd Bomb Group, based at Hardwick, England. Among other feats, "Joisey Bounce" flew on the Ploesti Raid on August 1, 1943. It was destroyed in a midair collision and its crew killed during a mission against Bremen, Germany, on November 13, 1943. *National Archives*

Consolidated B-24D-75-CO serial number 42-40597 is the closest of three B-24Ds flying in formation in an undated photograph. Two of the planes have the national white-star-in-blue-circle national insignia authorized from May 1942 to June 1943, while the center Liberator, B-24D-1-CF 42-63756 has an unusual national insignia similar to the one used from June to August 1943, with a red border but yellow instead of white side bars.

In a dramatic illustration of the strength of the Davis wings of the B-24D as well as an illuminating scale representation of the size of the plane, fifty-one men are standing from wingtip to wingtip. This Liberator is finished in bare aluminum and bears the national insignia authorized from August 1943 until after the end of World War II.

The prewar-type national insignia on the fuselage of this early-production B-24D taxiing at Wright Field, Ohio, narrows down the date to sometime between the first deliveries of this model in February 1942 and May of that year, when the new insignia without the red circle was introduced. In the background are a P-38, P-39, A-20, and B-26. This plane lacks the left cheek window with .50-caliber machine gun mount. *National Archives*

Consolidated B-24D-CO 40-2352 is viewed close-up from the front left in a photograph taken at an unidentified airfield on July 28, 1943. At this point in the B-24's development, there was only one .50-caliber machine gun installed in the nose. This provided scant protection from oncoming fighter planes, and soon more machine-gun mounts would be added to the nose in the form of cheek machine guns.

The fuselage of B-24D-CO serial number 40-2352 appears to be almost dragging on the ground in this photograph taken to the front of the plane. The prominent masts for the pitot tubes, a little more than midway above the sides of the nose, would later be moved up and to the rear once cheek machine guns were installed on the Liberators.

Early-production B-24Ds had a single .50-caliber "tunnel" gun, in the belly in the aft fuselage. It was an ineffective means of defense, so beginning with B-24D-CO 41-11587, a retractable, remote-controlled Bendix turret with two .50-caliber machine guns was mounted in the belly. The gunner, sitting above the turret, operated it using a periscope and hand controls, but the turret proved to be impractical and was discontinued.

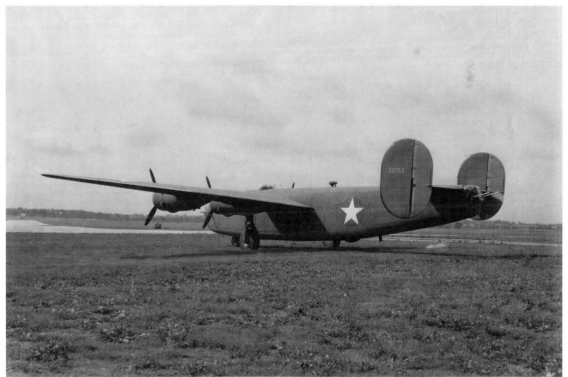

Consolidated B-24D-CO serial number 40-2352 was a very early D-model Liberator, being the fourth one produced. The tail turret is the early-type Consolidated A-6 model. In simple terms, in the early Consolidated tail turrets, the receivers of the machine guns were exposed; in later tail turrets, the receivers were enclosed.

The ultimate solution to the problem of Liberator defense against attacks from below was the Sperry ball turret. Armed with two .50-caliber machine guns, the turret had a 360-degree traverse and could be depressed to -90 degrees. The gunner sat in a scrunched-up position inside the turret; this arrangement proved much more effective than the remote-controlled belly turret. Here, civilian technicians inspect a retractable Sperry ball turret on a B-24D-CO. The access door to the turret was on the rear, hinged at the bottom.

This man demonstrates the tight squeeze to enter and exit the Sperry ball turret: but note, the gunner did not enter the turret until the Liberator was in the air, and he made sure to exit the turret, if possible, before landing. The unit is in the lowered position and is almost touching the ground: this was the reason why the ball turret was retractable in the B-24s. *Stan Piet collection*

A B-24D-CO is undergoing work by members of the 347th Sub-Depot, an airbase at Dodge City, Kansas (the name of the base is stenciled on the air compressor below the right wing). The red-bordered national insignia was the design authorized between June and August 1943, which helps to narrow down the date of this photograph. *National Archives*

A 1942 Autocar U-7144-T 4-5-ton 4x4 cab-over tractor with a tanker semitrailer and tanker trailer hitched in tandem is parked in front of two B-24D Liberators at an unidentified base in the summer of 1943. The second B-24D-145-CO in line is serial number 42-41195. *National Archives*

B-24D with no identifying markings is parked at Hensley Field, Dallas, Texas, during June 1942. On top of the fuselage to the front of the cockpit windscreen, and closer to the rear of the top of the clear nose, is the astrodome, a new feature introduced with the D-model Liberators. *Stan Piet collection*

A Consolidated A-6 tail turret is viewed close-up from the left side during World War II, illustrating the exposed receivers of the Browning M2 .50-caliber machine guns. The tail gunner sat in the turret between the two machine guns and had a flat plate of glass through which to operate his gun sight. In the small fairing on the tail below the turret are bomb-signal lights, to alert aircraft to the rear when this plane was releasing bombs. *National Archives*

The tail gunner's face is faintly visible through the flat window in this Consolidated A-6 turret. Muzzle compensators, which acted to reduce the vibration of the guns when firing, are attached to the ends of the barrels of the .50-caliber machine guns.
National Archives

"The Goon," B-24D-20-CI 41-24183, was named after, and decorated with a bomb-wielding likeness of, a character from the *Popeye* cartoons. This plane had the cheek machine guns moved to a new window just aft of the clear nose. While assigned to the 374th Bomb Squadron, 308th Bomb Group, based at Chengkung Airfield in China, this Liberator flew at least twenty-four combat missions. On the final one, a raid on Kowloon Docks near Hong Kong, "The Goon" experienced engine trouble, and seven of the ten crewmen bailed out. The three remaining crewmen were able to bring "The Goon" back to China; of the seven who bailed out, all but two were rescued. *National Archives*

Finished in bare aluminum, B-24D-135-CO serial number 42-41097, assigned to the 308th Bomb Group, flies over an airbase somewhere in the China-Burma-India (CBI) Theater in December 1944. On the ground are C-46 and C-47 transport planes and a column of horse carts transporting supplies.

This B-24D was one of the thirteen Liberators attached to the Halverson Detachment (HALPRO), a US heavy-bombardment unit based in Palestine beginning in mid-1942. There is a nickname on the side of the nose, but it is illegible. To the rear of that name is the emblem of the 8th Air Force. The national insignia dates the photograph to the summer of 1943 or later. The HALPRO detachment disbanded on October 31, 1942, when it became the 376th Bomb Group.

"Wash's Tub," B-24D-CO 41-11636, was one of the B-24s that served with HALPRO in 1942, and went on to operate with the "Liberandos," the 514th Bomb Squadron, 376th Bomb Group, in the North Africa Campaign. The plane is seen here with its flight crew during a Stateside war-bond drive. A chart showing "Wash's Tub's" travels was affixed to the side of the fuselage. *National Archives*

On August 1, 1943, B-24s from five USAAF bomb groups carried out a low-level bombing mission against the oil refineries at Ploesti, Romania, in an attempt to disrupt the flow of fuel to the Axis powers. At that time, the Ploesti refineries were producing almost one quarter of the Axis' petroleum. In this photo, Liberators are flying low over a US camp in Libya on a practice run prior to the Ploesti operation.

A member of the 376th Bomb Group cleans the clear nose of "Doodlebug," B-24D-1-CO serial number 41-23724, as the flight crew prepares to take off on the Ploesti raid on the morning of August 1, 1943. This Liberator had a .50-caliber machine gun in the lower nose, and the muzzle of a .50-caliber machine gun in the cheek position is visible next to the back of the man on the ladder.

A formation of low-flying B-24Ds were photographed from high above in a Liberator of the 389th Bomb Group as they were making their way to the oil refineries at Ploesti, on August 1, 1943. The bombers made their approach to the targets at low level in order to avoid detection by German radar.

Refinery facilities are exploding in the background as four B-24Ds from the 415th Bomb Squadron, 98th Bomb Group "Pyramiders" make a low-level run toward the group of refineries at the White IV area at Ploesti, on August 1, 1943. The closest Liberator is B-24D-1-CF 43-63758, nicknamed "Li'l Jughaid."

Thick, black smoke provides the backdrop for "The Sandman," B-24D-55-CO 42-40402, as it makes a run over the Astra Romana Refinery at Ploesti. A photographer in the tail of "Chug-a-Lug," another B-24D, snapped this photo.

Another target of the B-24s at Ploesti was the Columbia Aguilla Refinery. This photo, taken from a Liberator during the August 1, 1943, attack, shows how some of the oil tanks and walls of the refinery were painted in a squiggle camouflage pattern.

At the upper right, a B-24D with the 98th Bomb Group races over the Astra Romana Refinery at Ploesti. In the background, numerous fires and explosions from an earlier wave of Liberators created a thick pall of black smoke through which the following wave had to navigate. This smoke created serious problems for the bombardiers as they attempted to acquire their targets in their bombsights.

Four B-24Ds are faintly visible at the upper right and upper center as they run the gauntlet over the Astra Romana Refinery. In addition to having to contend with smoke, explosions, and unpredictably timed secondary explosions, the bombers and crews faced stiff opposition from Romanian and German flak gunners.

12

As seen from the tail of a Liberator, a formation of low-flying B-24Ds from the 44th Bomb Group, commanded by Col. Leon W. Johnson, are approaching in the background, silhouetted against the sky, as fires burn below in the Columbia Aquila Refinery. Col. Johnson was awarded the Congressional Medal of Honor for his conduct in the attack.

The Steaua Romana Refinery at Campina, Romania, was the target of two attacks on August 1, 1943. This view of the refinery under bombardment apparently was taken from a window in the right rear fuselage of one of the B-24Ds; note the bottom of the engine nacelle and the supercharger near its rear, at the top of the photo. The attack on this refinery placed it out of production for the remainder of the war.

Two B-24Ds from the 376th Bomb Group, Ninth Air Force, have just returned to an airbase near Benghazi, Libya, after the Ploesti raid. "Teggie Ann," B-24D-85-CO 42-40664, the plane of the group's commander, Col. Keith Compton, is the closer of the two Liberators. This plane bore the number "100" in white on the nose and the insignia and legend of the "Liberandos" below the cockpit. The plane in the background is numbered "81" on the nose.

"Kitty Quick," B-24D-CO 41-11630 from the 515th Bomb Squadron, 376th Bomb Group, rolls to a stop in a cloud of dust at a base near Benghazi, Libya, upon returning from the Ploesti raid. The number "83" is painted on the tail and on the nose. Another Liberator is faintly visible in the left background.

"Chum VII" was a B-24D-53-CO, serial number 42-40392, assigned to the 515th Bomb Squadron. It was camouflaged in Sand over Neutral Gray paint: the latter is visible on the raised bomb-bay doors. This aircraft was destroyed in a crash at El Batam, Tunisia, on August 13, 1943. Compare the revised location and design of the ball-and-socket mount for the cheek machine gun with that of B-24C 40-2384, seen earlier in this book. *Stan Piet collection*

The Oklahoma City Depot, Tinker Field, Oklahoma, performed a special modification on a number of B-24Ds, removing the glass nose and installing a revised nose incorporating a nose turret, windows for the bombardier in the chin, and revised windows for the navigator. These modified Liberators, of which sixty-seven reportedly were converted at Oklahoma City, were designated B-24D1 and nicknamed "Droop-snoots." This example displays the radically altered appearance these modifications occasioned. The nose turret is the Consolidated A-6A.

One of the B-24Ds outfitted with an Oklahoma City Depot modification was "White Savage," converted from B-24D-115-CO 42-40921. This Liberator was assigned to the 479th Antisubmarine Group in the UK, and it is painted in an antisubmarine camouflage scheme. Weatherproof covers are secured over the cockpit canopy and the nose turret and machine guns.

Barely visible on the nose of this Liberator with the Oklahoma City Depot nose is the nickname "Flash," with a thunderbolt painted below the name. This was B-24D-140-CO 42-41157, which served in the Aleutian Islands with the 404th Bomb Squadron, 28th Bomb Group. A large number "57" is present on the vertical fin but is difficult to discern because of the heavily weathered surfaces.

Tiger's head nose art has been painstakingly applied to this B-24D1. A large, yellow number "89" is painted to the rear of the nose art. This Liberator served in the 308th Bomb Group, 14th Air Force, which was active in China during World War II. *Stan Piet collection*

"Lulu's Ole Lady" was the nickname of this B-24D-50-CO, serial number 42-40328, photographed at Gander, Newfoundland, while performing antisubmarine duty. The aircraft was painted in an antisubmarine scheme of Olive Drab over White. *Stan Piet collection*

This B-24D-50-CO, serial number 42-40340, serving with the 10th Antisubmarine Squadron, 45th Bomb Group, is parked at the airbase at Gander, Newfoundland. The camouflage is Olive Drab over White, but with a less pronounced wavy demarkation between the two colors than on the Liberator in the preceding photo. *Stan Piet collection*

At Shemya Army Air Force Base in the Aleutian Islands, one of the B-24Ds with the 404th Bomb Squadron, 28th Bomb Group, is running up its engines preparatory to takeoff. A large number "8" is painted on the side of the nose. Faintly visible under the wings and also on the top of the aft fuselage are air-to-surface-vessel radar antennas, and two other glass-nose Liberators are in the left and center background. Tents in the background attest to the primitive living conditions at the base.
National Museum of the United States Air Force

"The Squaw," B-24D-CO 41-11761, is flying over a desert mountain range, likely during the plane's stint with a war-bond drive in the United States. Previous to this tour, "The Squaw" had been a participant in the fabled August 1, 1943, Ploesti raid. On the fuselage to the front of the left wing is the emblem of the 98th Bomb Group; the nickname of that group, "PYRAMIDERS"; and a map showing the plane's various combat missions.

B-24D-155-CO serial number 42-72786, nicknamed "Ten-Hi," served with the 5th Bomb Group in the Southwestern Pacific. At the time this photo was taken, the pilot of "Ten-Hi" was 1st Lt. Burdon L. Davidson of the 23rd Bomb Squadron. The nose art, which actually was below the side windows of the canopy, was a depiction of a can-can dancer. The A-6A nose turret was installed as a field or depot modification. The Olive Drab paint on the turret and on the fuselage to the rear of the turret was fresher, and thus darker, than the faded OD paint on the rest of the fuselage.

Although the August 1, 1943, low-level raid on Ploesti was the most famous mission against the refineries in that area, there were subsequent B-24 missions against that strategically important target. The B-24 depicted here lost its right outer wing section during one such mission, when an airman who had bailed out from a Liberator above this one struck the wing. The plane then lost control, flipped over, and crashed.

Preserved today in the National Museum of the Untied States Air Force, in 1943 "Strawberry Bitch" was one of many Liberators resting at the rain-soaked 55th Service Squadron Depot. *National Museum of the United States Air Force*

"Strawberry Bitch," B-24D-160-CO 42-72843, served in the 512th Bomb Squadron, 376th Bomb Group. A veteran of fifty-six combat missions, over Greece in October 1943, she was badly shot up, requiring over ninety patches in her right elevator. When photographed at the 55th Service Squadron Depot, her port vertical tail had been removed for maintenance, likely to repair this damage. *National Museum of the United States Air Force*

"First Sergeant," B-24D-30-CO serial number 42-40127, is painted in polka dots for high visibility while serving as an assembly ship with the 754th Bomb Squadron, 458th Bomb Group, 8th Air Force, based at RAF Horsham St. Faith. Earlier, this Liberator was named "Thar She Blows Again" and was a veteran of the August 1, 1943, raid on Ploesti. Assembly ships, also called "Judas goats," were war-weary aircraft tasked with taking off before the other bombers on a mission and leading them into formation, whereupon the assembly ship would return to base. "First Sergeant" was destroyed on the ground after the accidental discharge of a flaregun inside the plane on May 27, 1944.

"First Sergeant" is shown while being painted as an assembly ship, with the forward part of the fuselage coated in white paint. The dark rectangle below the cockpit canopy was the scoreboard, including an extra-large bomb representing the August 1, 1943 mission to Ploesti. The scoreboard was preserved intact when the high-visibility paint job was applied to the plane.

"Pete the Pom Inspector" was another Liberator veteran of the August 1, 1943, Ploesti mission that was relegated to assembly-ship duty. This was B-24D-53-CO serial number 42-40370, formerly named "Heaven Can Wait." As an assembly ship, "Pete the Pom Inspector" served with the 467th Bomb Group. The nose art alongside the cockpit, featuring a cartoon of a pilot on an airplane with a telescope to his eye, was repeated on the right side.

Originally called "Ball of Fire" while serving in the North Africa Campaign, this B-24D later was dubbed "Barber Bob" and served as an assembly ship. The plane was painted in red, white, and yellow stripes. It is still wearing the national insignia used from May 1942 to June 1943. *Roger Freeman collection*

No doubt, the most famous of the Liberators was "Lady Be Good," B-24D-25-CO serial number 41-24301, of the 514th Bomb Squadron. During the return flight from a bombing mission against Naples, Italy, in the early hours of April 5, 1943, the crew became lost while trying to find their home base at Soluch, Libya, and crash-landed the plane in the Libyan desert. The discoveries of the wrecked but well-preserved plane in 1958 and the remains of eight of its nine crewmen in 1960 were major news events, and the story has been the subject of numerous books, articles, and television dramatizations. "Lady Be Good" is seen here from the air at the crash site, its fuselage broken in two.

"Lady Be Good" is viewed from the front at the crash site. The propellers were feathered on the three remaining engines on the plane; engine four had been wrenched from its mount in the crash. Wreckage in the foreground includes one of the landing gear.

The crew of "Lady Be Good" pose next to their plane. They are, left to right, 1st Lt. William J. Hatton, pilot; 2nd Lt. Robert F. Toner, copilot; 2nd Lt. D.P. Hays, navigator; 2nd Lt. John S. Woravka, bombardier; TSgt. Harold J. Ripslinger, flight engineer; TSgt. Robert E. LaMotte, radio operator; SSgt. Guy E. Shelley, gunner/ assistant flight engineer; SSgt. Vernon L. Moore, gunner/assistant radio operator; and SSgt. Samuel R. Adams, gunner. Their bombing mission to Naples, which began on April 4, 1943, would be their first and last mission together as a crew.

The Consolidated A-6 tail turret of "Lady Be Good" is shown here in the condition it was in when the aircraft was located. It was found that the guns of the plane were still in working condition, even after fifteen years of exposure in the desert.

Although the location of "Lady Be Good" was discovered and recorded by a British oil-exploration team in November 1958, it was not until May 1959 that a USAF recovery team visited the site. The plane had crashed 440 miles south of its base at Soluch. The plane is viewed from aft, with a C-47 that had brought a recovery team to the site visible in the background.

Members of the recovery crew are exploring the ruins of "Lady Be Good." Once the aircraft was located and investigated, there were no signs of the crewmen. It would not be until 1960 that fuller details of the fate of the crew would be discovered.

In a view of the upper deck of "Lady Be Good," the emergency escape hatch is open to the front of the dorsal turret. Toward the right, the hatch cover for the compartment containing two inflatable dinghies is ajar.

The interior of the aft part of the fuselage, which was torn away from the forward fuselage during the crash of "Lady Be Good," is viewed. In the foreground, the two waist windows are swung up in their open positions. Immediately aft of the waist windows were two ¼-inch armor panels, with just enough space to squeeze by in order to go to the rear of the fuselage.

"Strawberry Bitch," B-24D-160-CO 42-72843, served with the 512th Bomb Squadron, 376th Bomb Group, from September 1943 to April 1944. After the war, the plane was stored at Davis-Monthan Air Force Base, Arizona, and it is seen here in May 1959, preparing for its final flight, to Wright-Patterson Air Force Base, Ohio, where it was placed on display at the United States Air Force Museum. *National Archives*

With outer-wing panels removed to allow it clearance through the columns of the overpass in the background, "Strawberry Bitch" is being towed to the new United States Air Force Museum at Wright-Patterson Air Force Museum. To this day, this plane remains on static display indoors at the National Museum of the United States Air Force, as the institution subsequently was renamed. *National Archives*

With her outer wing panels back in place, "Strawberry Bitch" rests on the ramp just outside the new National Museum of the United States Air Force. *National Museum of the United States Air Force*

The nose wheel of "Strawberry Bitch" at the National Museum of the United States Air Force is seen from the right side. This wheel was designed to be steerable to 45 degrees to the left and right of center, but pilots were instructed never to turn it more than 30 degrees in either direction. This wheel was fitted with a 36-inch, 10-ply tire. *Photo by author*

The left cheek machine gun and its ball-and-socket mount are the focus of this photo of "Strawberry Bitch." To the left is the side of the glass nose, and to the upper right is the strut that holds the left pitot tube. *Photo by author*

The small fender that protects the front landing gear bay from mud and debris is clearly visible. *Photo by author*

The cockpit of "Strawberry Bitch" is viewed through the copilot's side window. The pilot's seat is in the left background. Between the seats is the control pedestal; the four tall levers on the left front of the pedestal are the throttle controls, while the four shorter levers to the right are the fuel mixture controls. To the sides of the pedestal are the pilot's and copilot's control yokes. To the right is the instrument panel. *National Museum of the United States Air Force*

The control pedestal in the cockpit of "Strawberry Bitch" is viewed close-up. To the front of the pedestal are three groups of four levers each: from left to right, they are controls for the turbosuperchargers, the throttles, and fuel mixture. The round knob toward the rear of the top of the pedestal is the rudder tab control, while on the rear face of the pedestal, at the bottom of the photo, is the aileron tab control. *National Museum of the United States Air Force*

The cockpit is viewed from between the pilot's and copilot's seats. In the center foreground, on the control pedestal, are trim-control wheels, the command radio control box (bottom center), light switches, and cowl-flap switches. Rudder pedals and footrests are below the instrument panel. Above the center of the instrument panel is a cluster containing, from top to bottom, four red-colored propeller-feathering switches and a clock, and, from left to right, a remote indicating compass and a magnetic compass.
National Museum of the United States Air Force

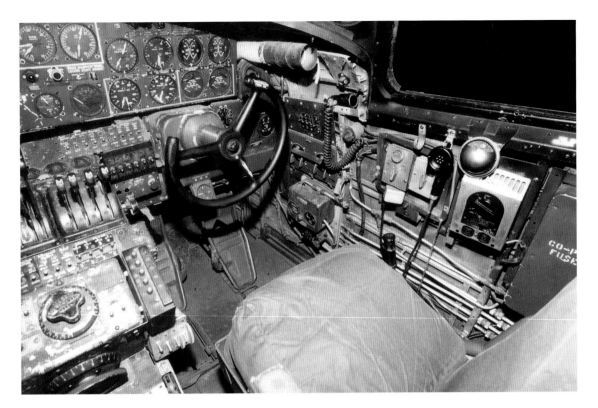

The copilot occupied the right side of the cockpit. Among the equipment on the side wall are the copilot's intercom control box, a hand microphone, the control box for his heated flight suit, and, to the far right, the copilot's fuse box. *National Museum of the United States Air Force*

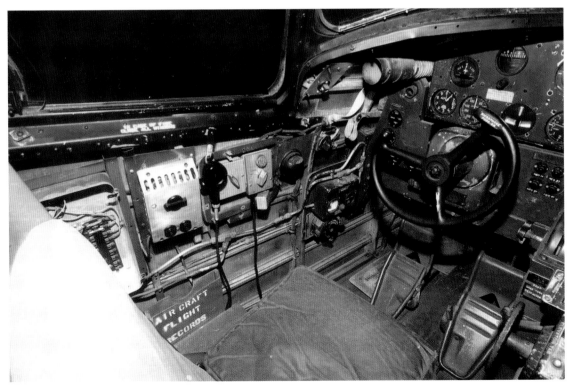

In a view of the pilot's side of the cockpit, to the left, partially hidden by the seat, is the pilot's fuse box, to the front of which are a bin for flight records; the control box for his heated flight suit; a hand mike; intercom controls; and, to the left of the control yoke, the pilot's oxygen control box. *National Museum of the United States Air Force*

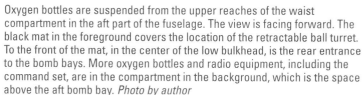

Oxygen bottles are suspended from the upper reaches of the waist compartment in the aft part of the fuselage. The view is facing forward. The black mat in the foreground covers the location of the retractable ball turret. To the front of the mat, in the center of the low bulkhead, is the rear entrance to the bomb bays. More oxygen bottles and radio equipment, including the command set, are in the compartment in the background, which is the space above the aft bomb bay. *Photo by author*

In the waist compartment, looking forward, to the right are the right .50-caliber waist machine gun and a flexible feed chute for .50-caliber ammunition. To the lower left, a black mat covers the location of the well for the retractable ball turret. *Photo by author*

The left waist machine gun is visible through the left waist window. The frame the gun is mounted on is an E13 Adapter, which formed in effect a cradle for the gun, and also held the gun sight and the hand grips. To the left of center is the wind deflector, which prevented the brunt of the airflow from pouring into the open waist window. *Photo by author*

The left waist window is viewed from a different angle, showing the inner frame of the window, which is coated in a greenish zinc chromate primer. Also visible are the two operating arms of the wind deflector, which fit into slots in the fuselage skin. *Photo by author*

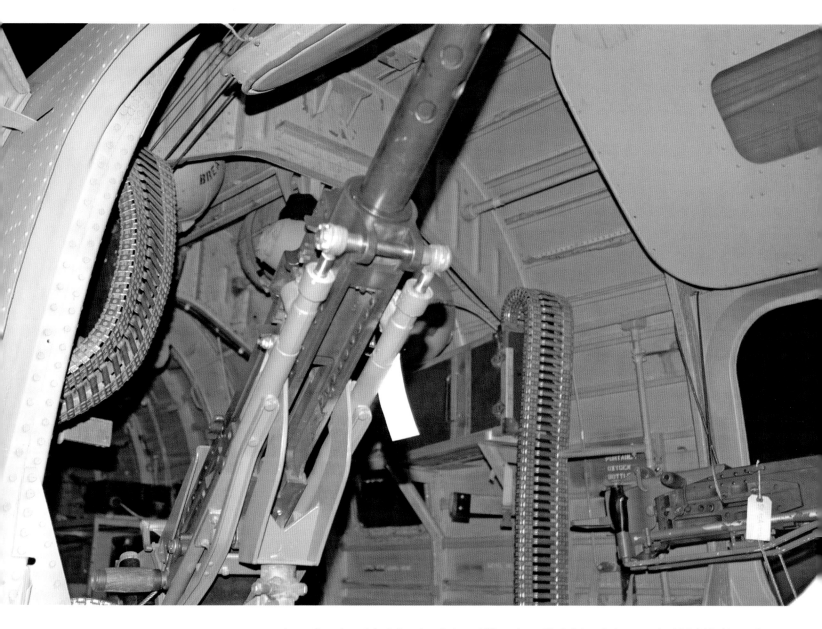

In another view of the left waist window of "Strawberry Bitch," the window panel, which folded inward when opened, is visible in the upper part of the compartment to the left of the machine-gun barrel. To the upper right is the right waist window panel in the open position. The manner in which the E13 Adapter is pinned to the two lugs on the bottom front of the machine-gun receiver is apparent. Also in view at the lower center is the ammunition box for the right waist machine gun. *Photo by author*

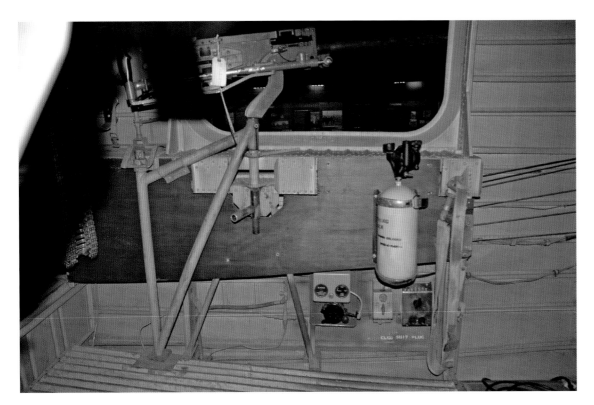

The right waist machine gun and its mount are viewed through the left waist window of "Strawberry Bitch." The gun is mounted on a swiveling pedestal. Below the yellow portable oxygen bottle are, left to right, the right waist gunner's oxygen regulator, intercom control, and flight-suit heater control box. *Photo by author*

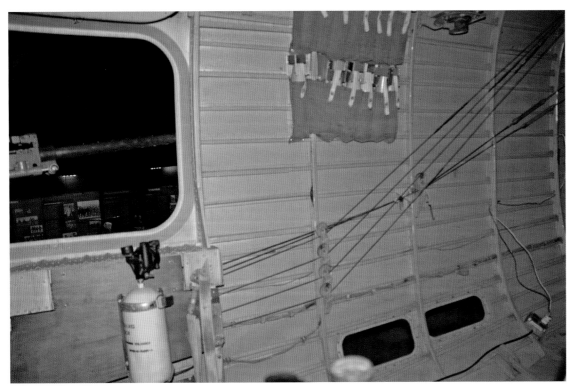

The area from the right waist window (left) aft to the two small observation windows low on the fuselage (lower right) is illustrated. Note the control cables for the right rudder and elevator, including their guide pulleys above the forward of the two observation windows. *Photo by author*

In a view from the waist of the fuselage of "Strawberry Bitch" looking aft, there are two narrow catwalks leading to the tail turret, the aft catwalk being higher than the forward one. Control cables are visible overhead and on the right side of the fuselage (left in the photo). *Photo by author*

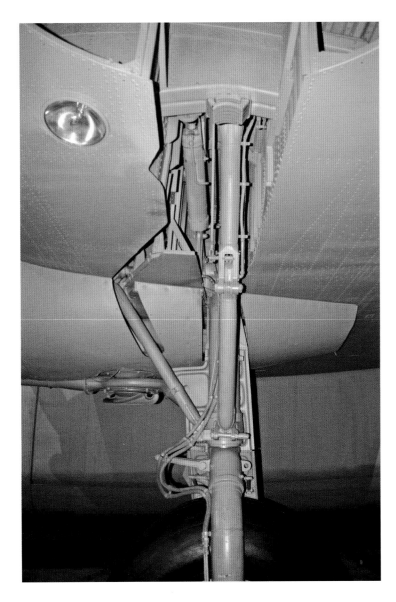

The main-gear wheels (the left one is seen from the outboard side) were Air Corps Type 111, constructed of aluminum-alloy or magnesium-alloy castings, and were mounted with 56-inch, 16-ply tires. *Photo by author*

The left main landing gear is viewed from outboard, with the wheel well in the bottom of the wing at the top. The tops of the main, or oleo, strut and the diagonal drag brace are attached to pivoting mounts in the rear of the engine nacelle, with cutouts in the nacelle to accommodate these structures. At the upper left is the left landing light. *Photo by author*

The right main wheel of "Strawberry Bitch" is seen from its inboard side. The brake line emerges from the hollow axle at the center of the wheel. The bottom of the landing-gear door is next to the top of the wheel. *Photo by author*

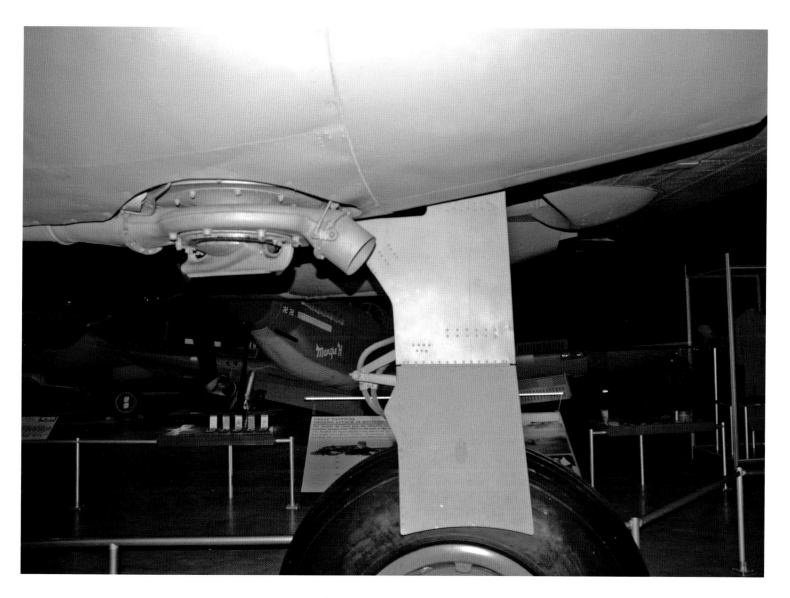

The rear of the right engine nacelle and the exposed part of the right turbosupercharger are depicted, as well as the upper part of the right main landing-gear door. The parts of the exhaust and turbosupercharger system that are in view are, from left to right, the exhaust tailpipe, the turbosupercharger assembly, and the exhaust waste gate. *Photo by author*

As part of a deal to enable the US Navy to operate land-based bombers for long-range maritime patrol, reconnaissance, and attack purposes, beginning in 1942, the US Army Air Forces transferred to the Navy a total of 977 B-24s that the Navy designated PB4Y-1s. (In return, the Air Forces obtained the use of the Navy's aircraft factory at Renton, Washington, for the manufacture of B-29 Superfortress bombers.) The early PB4Y-1s were derived from B-24Ds. The example shown here was nicknamed "Calvert & Coke," US Navy Bureau Number (BuNo) 32032. It served with Bombing Squadron 103 (VB-103) and had a yellow, retractable radome in the belly. *National Archives*

PB4Y-1 BuNo 32059 was an example from the first of seven blocks of BuNos assigned to the PB4Y-1s. It bears the US recognition insignia adopted in mid-August 1943, consisting of a white star on a blue circle, with white side bars bordered in blue. Two .50-caliber machine guns are protruding from the nose. The original label for this photograph implies that this is a Marine PB4Y-1, and explains that a Marine PB4Y-1 was the first US aircraft to photograph the Japanese naval base at Truk.

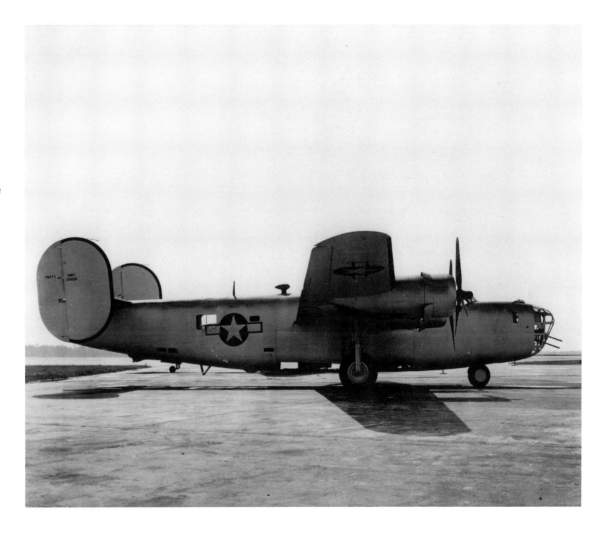

PB4Y-1 BuNo 31995 is parked at an unidentified airbase and is marked with the national insignia that was authorized from May 1942 to June 1943. The tail skid is lowered; this helped protect the bottoms of the vertical fins during nose-high landings.

"Calvert & Coke," PB4Y-1 BuNo 32032 and code B-3, cruises low over the ocean during a patrol mission. During a night patrol mission on November 12, 1943, "Calvert & Coke" was shot down by the German U-boat U-508, and the entire crew of the PB4Y-1 was lost. However, the plane managed to sink the U-boat.

Two officers examine a KDN-1 target drone on a stand next to a US Navy PB4Y-1 assigned to the Naval Modification Unit in Johnsville, Pennsylvania, in the immediate postwar era. The KDN-1 was powered by a small turbojet engine and could reach speeds up to 500 miles per hour. The PB4Y-1 was used as a mother ship to carry the KDN-1s aloft. *Stan Piet collection*

CHAPTER 8
Liberator III/GR. V

The Liberator III was the designation for the 156 B-24Ds acquired by the British. The Liberator IIIs differed from the B-24Ds in several respects: in most Liberator IIIs the Boulton-Paul four-gun tail turrets replaced the Consolidated tail turrets; planes retaining the original Consolidated tail turrets were designated Liberator IIIA. Here, British Liberators, including two No.120 Squadron Liberator IIIs in the foreground, FK228 and FL933, are parked on a flight line at RAF Aldergrove, Northern Ireland, during April 1943. Both of these Liberators have radar antennas on the noses, under the wings, and on the sides of the waist area of the fuselage. The third aircraft in line is a Liberator GR. V with a chin radome. *Imperial War Museum*

Still seeking to augment its bomber force, the British acquired their own version of the B-24D through Lend-Lease. The RAF aircraft, designated Liberator Mark III, were not identical to their American counterparts. In each waist position was installed a pair of .303 Browning machine guns, with the same type of weapon in the nose. Most were equipped with Boulton-Paul rear turrets, armed with four .303-caliber Browning machine guns, rather than the Consolidated A-6A turrets installed at the rear of a B-24D. The handful of aircraft that were equipped with the Consolidated turret and its pair of Browning .50-caliber machine guns bore the designation Liberator Mk. IIIA.

The RAF obtained 156 Liberator IIIs and assigned them serial numbers BZ833 through BZ860; BZ890 through BZ909; BZ922 through BZ929; BZ932 through BZ936; BZ946 through BZ959; FK214 through FK245; FL906 through FL926; FL928 through FL936; FL939, FL940, FL943, FL945, and FL992 through FL995; and LV336 through LV346.

The British also acquired another B-24D derivative, which was designated the Liberator GR. Mark V. Like many of the RAF Liberators that preceded them, these 210 aircraft were outfitted for antisubmarine patrols. The bombers so equipped had Air-to-Surface Vessel (ASV) radar, which were used in conjunction with Leigh Lights. The ASV unit was typically mounted in a chin fairing beneath the nose.

The Leigh Light, a carbon arc searchlight, was extremely powerful and highly effective. The version mounted in a nacelle beneath the wing of the Liberator was thirty-two inches in diameter and had a maximum beam intensity of 90 million candles. An operator in the bomber could rotate the light electrically fifty degrees to either side of center and forty-eight degrees down from horizontal.

Ground crewmen at RAF Beaulieu, England, are performing a routine inspection of a Liberator III assigned to No.224 Squadron during December 1942. The four-gun Boulton-Paul tail turret is visible. Liberators assigned to antisubmarine and anti-shipping duties usually carried white paint on their sides and bottoms. *Imperial War Museum*

Some Liberator Mark IIIs assigned to RAF Coastal Command were equipped with ventral radomes for use in anti-shipping operations, and they were designated Liberator GR. V. One such plane is shown here, serial number BZ877, serving with RAF's No.86 Squadron based in Northern Ireland in 1943. *Imperial War Museum*

At RAF Aldergrove, Northern Ireland, two Liberators of No. 86 Squadron are in view. The closer one is Liberator GR. IIIA serial number LV345: note the twin-machine-gun Consolidated tail turret and the retracted ventral radome aft of the rear bomb bay. The Liberator in the distance bears fuselage code M. *Imperial War Museum*

This Liberator GR Mk. III, serial number FK222, photographed at Scottish Aviation Ltd. at Prestwick, while undergoing modifications in August 1942, wears the white-camouflaged sides and undersides of antisubmarine aircraft. The aircraft was assigned successively to the Nos. 120 and 86 Squadrons, RAF, and No. 1332 Conversion Unit.

Seen in flight is a Liberator III armed with four 3-inch high-velocity aircraft rockets (HVARs) on stub wings installed on each side of the fuselage below the cockpit. These, in combination with the aircraft's bombs and air-to-surface-vessel radar (antennas are present on the nose, rear fuselage, and wing bottoms), made the plane a potent submarine killer.

Another tool in the Liberator III's antisubmarine and anti-shipping repertoire was the Leigh Light, a very powerful 20-inch-diameter searchlight carried in a pod under a wing. The Leigh Light generated a beam of up to 90 million candles, enabling the Liberator crew to visually lock on targets on the blackest nights. The light element was behind a clear Plexiglas lens, which a crewman is buffing here. *Imperial War Museum*

A Type C rocket-launcher installation is viewed on the left side of an RAF Liberator III. Four launcher rails with rockets mounted are on the underside of the stub wing. Two tubular braces to the fuselage help stabilize the stub wing.

During April 1943, a ground crewman is cleaning the bore of one of the Browning .303-caliber machine guns on a Boulton-Paul tail turret on a Liberator III serving with No.120 Squadron at RAF Aldergrove. In the background is Liberator III serial number FL906, with fuselage code J. *Imperial War Museum*

During World War II, the British converted quantities of B-24Ds/Liberator IIIs to Liberator GR. Vs, for service with RAF Coastal Command. Some nineteen GR. Vs were diverted to the Royal Canadian Air Force (RCAF). The GR. Vs featured an air-to-surface-vessel (ASV) radar, either in a fixed radome under the chin, or in a retractable radome in the belly of the plane aft of the bomb bay. The Liberator GR. Vs operated with ten squadrons: Nos.53, 59, 86, 120, 160, 200, 220, 311, 354, and 547. The example shown here has the chin radome. Note the placement of a machine gun in the center of the nose.

A Liberator GR. V with fuselage code G and a chin radome runs up its engines at an unidentified airbase. The GR. Vs often were painted in dark colors, likely shades of gray and green, on the upper surfaces, and white on the sides and undersides. A number, apparently "590" but possibly "598," is faintly visible on the upper front of the radome: both of these numbers coincided with the serial numbers of two of the RCAF Liberator GR Vs.

A three-digit number is painted on the upper front of the chin radome of this RAF Coastal Command Liberator GR. V: the first two numbers are "7" and "2," which are consistent with the numeric parts of a number of RAF Liberator GR Vs. *Stan Piet collection*

CHAPTER 9
C-87

Ever since the LB-30As, the Liberators had been proven to lend themselves well to conversion to transport aircraft, because of their extended range, powerful engines, capacity for fuel, and commodious fuselages. Ultimately, Consolidated Fort Worth produced 287 examples of a long-range, high-altitude, high-capacity transport based on the B-24D, called the C-87 Liberator Express. The example shown here, USAAF serial number 42-40355, was given the nickname "Pinocchio" and had nose art of the famed wooden puppet, sporting an extra-long nose.

Owing to the tremendous shortage of transport aircraft with long range and heavy lift capacity early in World War II, it is not surprising that the Liberator was adapted to that role as well. The new variant, officially designated the C-87, was given the name Liberator Express. Consolidated's Fort Worth plant was the sole producer of the cargo variant, production of which began on September 2, 1942. The impetus of this was the repair of B-24D serial number 42-40355, which had been heavily damaged while landing. The bomber was rebuilt into a transport configuration, with a cargo door in place of the bombardier's characteristic glass nose. A second, larger door was cut into the left fuselage behind the wing, and all armament was removed. Seating for twenty-five passengers was installed.

Following the evaluation of that first transport aircraft at Bolling Field, an order was placed for more examples. So pressing was the demand for transports in 1942, that the first seventy-three C-87s were converted from B-24Ds. Production of the type continued until August 10, 1944, by which time 287 had been built.

While the Air Transport Command operated many of the C-87s, they were joined by contracted commercial carriers as well, including, not surprisingly, Consolidated's subsidiary Corsairways, who flew the type in the Pacific. Additionally, American Airlines flew the Liberator Express on North and South Atlantic routes, and United Air Lines flew them on Transpacific as well as Australia and New Zealand intra-theater routes. In the South Atlantic, the C-87 was flown by Transcontinental and Western Airlines—later known as TWA. Regardless of operator, the handling and performance of the C-87 was not well liked, hence the type was retired as quantities of the Douglas C-54 were delivered.

Consolidated C-87 Liberator Express serial number 41-23904 is parked on a snowy hardstand. The Liberator Express featured a solid nose, which retained the general shape of the glass nose on the bomber version but was hinged on one side. There were seven rectangular windows on each side of the midsection of the fuselage. A door measuring six by six feet was installed on the left side of the fuselage in the area of the national insignia. *National Archives*

C-87 41-23904 is seen from the left rear. In lieu of the tail turret of the bomber version was a plain metal tail enclosure. Consolidated's Fort Worth plant manufactured the C-87s between September 1942 and August 1944. Existing B-24Ds were converted to the first seventy-three C-87s, while the remaining 214 were built from scratch. *National Archives*

The same C-87, serial number 41-23904, is viewed from the left front. A rectangular window was installed in the nose. Seats for twenty-five passengers were installed in the fuselage. Air Transport Command operated the C-87s, but four civilian airlines also assisted in operating them: American Airlines, Consairways, Transcontinental & Western Air, and United Air Lines. *National Archives*

All four engines are warming up in this frontal view of a Consolidated C-87 Liberator Express. In the C-87, the navigator was stationed aft of the cockpit, and he had an astrodome overhead, which is faintly visible in this photo above the cockpit canopy. *Stan Piet collection*

Civilian personnel are preparing four early-production C-87s for delivery. In the foreground is C-87 serial number 41-11674. The national insignia on the second plane is the type in use from May 1942 to June 1943. *Library of Congress*

CHAPTER 10
XB-41

In the first part of 1943, as the Allies were ramping up the air war against Germany, the US Army Air Forces lacked long-range fighter planes to escort the strategic bombers on long-range missions. Thus, the Army Air Forces conducted experiments with B-17s and a single B-24, fitted out with extra .50-caliber machine-gun turrets. It was hoped that sending these gunships with bomber formations would provide enough additional firepower to protect the formations. The Liberator selected for the experiments was B-24D-CO serial number 41-11822, and the conversion was designated XB-41. Key features were a redesigned glass nose; a chin turret; a raised dorsal turret; a new, additional dorsal turret farther aft; and twin machine guns in Plexiglas enclosures in the waist positions. *American Aviation Historical Society*

The US strategy of precision daylight bombing in Europe came with a heavy cost, especially early in the war, and it increased substantially as the formations of bombers plunged deeper over German territory. While later in the war, long-range fighters, notably the P-38 Lightning, P-47 Thunderbolt, and notably the P-51 Mustang, could escort the bomber formations to the target and back, that was not the case in 1942.

At that time, no allied fighter had range capabilities approaching that of the bombers. In an effort to compensate, the Army Air Force experimented with fitting out some bombers as "gunships" to protect the bomber formations on long flights over enemy territory.

As part of this effort, Liberator 41-11822, a B-24D, was selected for modification to XB-41 gunship configuration. The armament of the Liberator was significantly increased; pairs of .50-caliber machine guns were mounted in each waist position, and on top of the aircraft a second turret augmented the standard B-24D top unit. Beneath the nose was fitted a Bendix chin turret. In sum, the XB-41 now boasted no less than fourteen heavy machine guns.

To supply all those barrels with lead, the aircraft was filled with 12,420 rounds of ammunition, which pushed the takeoff weight of the aircraft to 63,000 pounds, only 2,000 pounds below the upper limit for the airframe. The bomb bay was modified to store 4,000 of the 12,420 rounds of ammunition, where it was held in reserve.

The sole XB-41 was delivered to Eglin Field, Florida, on January 29, 1943, for testing. After two months of testing, on March 21, 1943, the XB-41 was declared unfit for operational use. Flight tests had indicated that the aircraft, which had increased drag owning to the additional turrets and barrels, and was heavily burdened with ammunition, struggled to reach the altitude that bomber formations were expected to operate at. The heavily taxed engines were prone to overheating. Consolidated attempted to address these problems by changing propellers and removing some of the armor plating, but additional testing at Eglin in July 1943 indicated many problems remained. Further, similarly modified Flying Fortresses, the YB-40, undergoing service testing in Europe revealed a significant flaw in the gunship strategy. The bomber aircraft, be they B-17 or B-24, once relieved of the burden of their bomb load over the target, would quickly hurry toward safer skies. The gunships, however, had only been relieved of a portion of their payload through aerial combat, and could not keep up with the bombers they were supposed to be escorting! Accordingly, work on the XB-41 project ceased, and the XB-41 was redesignated as TB-24D and used to train mechanics until it was finally scrapped at Maxwell Field, Alabama, on February 2, 1945.

A Bendix chin turret with twin .50-caliber machine guns was installed under the nose of the XB-41. A gunner stationed above the turret controlled it remotely. The turret is shown here traversed to the left. The glazed nose was redesigned, with the upper half being of a semi-dome shape without frames to obscure the gunner's view. *American Aviation Historical Society*

The Plexiglas enclosure is present in this photograph of the left waist machine-gun mount of the XB-41. It was discovered during tests that these enclosures interfered with the gunners' vision and ability to aim the guns. *American Aviation Historical Society*

The forward dorsal turret of the XB-41 could be lowered, as seen here, in order to reduce drag. In the raised position, it was better able to fire over the aft dorsal turret. The windscreen and the raised coaming around the front, top, and bottom of the redesigned waist window are visible; the Plexiglas enclosure for the twin machine guns has been removed from the waist window. *American Aviation Historical Society*

The heavily armed XB-41 rests on a concrete ramp next to a stock Liberator. The under slung, B-17G-style chin turret, elevated forward upper turret, and barely visible rear upper turret gave the gunship a distinctive appearance. *American Aviation Historical Society*

The Consolidated F-7 was a long-range, high-altitude photo-reconnaissance aircraft based on the B-24D. The first of these, 41-11653, was converted at Lowry Air Base, Colorado. This was followed by a handful of additional aircraft converted at the Northwest Airlines Modification Center, St. Paul, Minnesota. These planes had three trimetrogon cameras just aft of the nose, which were capable of taking panoramic, horizon-to-horizon reconnaissance photographs, and other reconnaissance cameras were mounted in the belly of the plane further aft. In this in-flight view of "Hi Doc," Consolidated F-7 serial number 41-11598, the camera ports are visible in the belly aft of the bomb bays. Two names are present on the right side of the fuselage: "Hi Doc," with "Bugs Bunny" nose art, and, aft of the waist window, "Sally Lou," with pinup art of a woman on a swing.

In a close-up view of "Hi Doc," F-7 serial number 41-11598, the small window for the left camera in the trimetrogon suite is visible on the fuselage to the front of the nose wheel. The two outboard cameras were oblique, while the center one was vertical. Although the F-7s were reconnaissance aircraft, and had no bombing equipment, they were fully armed with machine guns and turrets.

As seen in a photo of the left side of the nose of "Hi Doc," the nose art was the same on each side, except the cartoon image of "Bugs Bunny" was the mirror image from side to side, with his ears pointing to the front of the aircraft. Note the window for the left trimetrogon camera below the white towel to the immediate rear of the crewman.

Two camera operators are at work inside a Consolidated F-7 during a mission over Leyte in the Philippines. The camera in the right foreground is a Fairchild K-18 Aerial Camera, suitable for medium- to high-altitude reconnaissance. It produced 9″x18″ negatives, with a 24-inch/f6 focal length. In addition to the three trimetrogon cameras in the nose, the F-7s carried as many as eight additional cameras in the bomb bay and aft fuselage.

"Ol' Nick" was an F-7 converted from B-24D-CO 41-11673. This plane was assigned to the 1st Photographic Squadron, 1st Photographic Group. This F-7 had a round port for the right oblique trimetrogon camera, visible below and aft of the letter Z on the nose. Above the "Ol' Nick" painted on the fuselage is a likeness of the devil inside a circle; for extra effect, a pitchfork is also part of the nose art (*Note*: "Ol' Nick" is an English nickname for the devil).

CHAPTER 12
B-24E

The final glass-nosed model of the Liberator, the B-24E, was a product of the Ford Motor Company and was manufactured under the Liberator Production Pool, an arrangement in which B-24 production was spread among several manufacturers and plants. Ford not only built complete B-24s at its new Willow Run plant in Michigan, but also produced subassemblies, which it shipped to the Consolidated plant in Fort Worth and the Douglas plant in Tulsa for final assembly. Seen here is B-24E-5-FO ("FO" being the suffix indicating that Ford produced the plane), serial number 42-7020. A white placard with the numbers "7020" over "40" is affixed to the side of the nose.

The B-24E was the last model of the so-called "glass-nose" Liberators produced. However, as the era of these classic early B-24s came to a close, a bold new chapter in the Liberator saga opened. As discussed previously, three plants, located in San Diego, Tulsa, and Fort Worth, were busily turning out the bombers—yet production could still not keep pace with demand.

Seeking to up production, the Ford Motor Company was contracted in 1941 to produce components to feed to the Douglas plant in Tulsa, and the Consolidated Fort Worth facility. The latter in particular would relieve pressure on the San Diego facility, which was supplying the components not only for its own production, but the Texas production as well. It was expected that production at all three plants would rise as a result of Ford manufacturing subassemblies.

A new plant was built outside of Detroit, in an area known as Willow Run. The massive new plant was a quarter mile wide and a half mile long, and was situated on a sixty-five-acre site. Ford, who had only modest prior experience manufacturing aircraft, sent a team of engineers to San Diego to observe the Liberator production process.

Subsequent to this visit, in October 1941, the Ford contract was modified such that Ford would not only provide subassemblies to Tulsa and Fort Worth, but would also assemble complete aircraft at Willow Run. Specially built tractor trailers would transport the components, including virtually complete fuselages, to the Tulsa and Fort Worth plants.

On May 15, 1942, the first Ford-assembled Liberator, B-24E 42-7770, rolled out of the Willow Run plant. Although assembled by Ford at Willow Run, this aircraft, referred to as the "educational ship," was produced in a manner almost reverse of its successors. The bulk of this aircraft's components were made by Consolidated in San Diego, and shipped to Willow Run for assembly. This aircraft was turned over to the USAAF Flight Department for acceptance on September 1, 1942.

The B-24E, while resembling a B-24D, lacked the belly turret found on the D. Internally, the B-24E incorporated several changes made in order to adapt the Liberator to the higher rates of production targeted by Ford.

That first aircraft was followed by serial number 42-6976, which was completed on September 10, 1942, using primarily Willow Run-produced components. Initial production was beset by various difficulties and delays. Although Ford would completely assemble only 490 of the 801 B-24Es produced (Consolidated assembling 167 in Tulsa and Douglas 144 in Fort Worth), the lessons learned by the automotive giant on these aircraft were important. While the B-24E was largely obsolete by the time they left the assembly line, and hence were used primarily for training purposes, Ford would carry on producing later models of the B-24, with the production rate soaring to one per hour.

A crew runs up the engines of brand-new B-24E 42-7011 outside Ford's Willow Run bomber plant. This bomber is a rare example of an aircraft with factory applied nose art—a rendering of famed World War I ace Eddie Rickenbacker—and carried as well not only his name, but his signature. Unfortunately, the aircraft, which was assigned to 391st Bomb Squadron, 34th Bomb Group was lost while on a training flight in California. Two of her crew were lost at sea, but the remaining eight bailed out over land and survived. *Library of Congress*

A mission completed, the crew of B-24E025-FO 42-7314 departs from their plane. The date, judging by the national insignia, was sometime between May 1942 and June 1943. From this angle, the flat plate of glass on the rear of the tail turret is visible; this flat plate gave the gunner an undistorted clear panel by which to aim his .50-caliber guns.

When an Army Air Forces aircraft was considered war-weary or unfit or unsuited for all of the purposes for which it was designed, it was assigned the prefix "R," for Restricted. Such was the case with this Ford-built Liberator, designated an RB-24E-26-FO. A close examination of the photo reveals that the national insignia (with side bars) on the fuselage, and a large number "341" on the nose, have been painted over.

Among the heavy bombers on a snowy flight line at an unidentified airbase are two Liberators, including, in the foreground, B-24E 42-6981. This is an interesting plane: its dorsal turret was removed and the opening faired over; the bottom of the clear nose was chopped off, and what appears to be a nose turret was installed. This may have been an experimental mounting of a Bendix chin turret, similar to the one that had been installed in the XB-41, discussed earlier in this book.

A trio of B-24s, with B-24E-5-FO serial number 42-7054 in the foreground, flies in formation over an unidentified landscape, likely in the United States. The tail numbers of the other two Liberators are indistinct: the plane to the front was not a B-24E, but it is possible, from what is visible of the tail number, that the farthest plane was a B-24E.

In a photograph symbolic of the United States' industrial might during World War II, Liberators as far as the eye can see are under construction at Consolidated's plant in Fort Worth, Texas. On the assembly line to the right is a mix of B-24Ds and B-24Es, while to the left, the first seven Liberators are painted in antisubmarine camouflage.